EDGE O

# THE RIVER

HEART OF

# THE CITY

*The sternwheelers W. Ogilvie, Australian and Nora docked at Canyon City, 1899.*
*Yukon Archives 3609/Barley Collection*

EDGE OF

# THE RIVER

HEART OF

# THE CITY

*A* HISTORY *of the* WHITEHORSE WATERFRONT

*by* The Yukon Historical & Museums Association

*researched & written by* Helene Dobrowolsky & Rob Ingram

Lost Moose Publishing
Whitehorse, Yukon
1994

Published by Lost Moose Publishing Ltd., 58 Kluane Crescent, Whitehorse, Yukon, Canada Y1A 3G7, phone (403) 668-5076, fax (403) 668-6223

**Canadian Cataloguing in Publication Data**
Dobrowolsky, Helene
  Edge of the river, heart of the city

  Includes bibliographical references.
  ISBN 0-9694612-2-4

  1. Whitehorse Waterfront (Yukon)--History. 2. Waterfronts--Yukon--Whitehorse--History  3. Whitehorse (Yukon)--History   I. Ingram, Rob   II. Yukon Historical & Museums Association   III. Title
  FC4046.4.D62 1994       971.9'1      C94-910358-6
  F1095.5.W5D62 1994

Photographs in this book are reprinted with permission
Illustrations by Rob Ingram
Design by Rice Advertising, Whitehorse, Yukon
Production by K-L Services, Whitehorse, Yukon

Printed and bound in Canada

# TABLE OF CONTENTS

# ACKNOWLEDGMENTS

The research and writing of the original waterfront study was sponsored by the Government of the Yukon, Department of Economic Development, Community Development Fund in 1992. The Yukon government's Department of Tourism, Heritage Branch, printed the initial study and, in 1993/94, provided funding support for the development of this book.

This history relied heavily on the work of those who have come before. An invaluable aid was the collection of Whitehorse building files compiled by Len Tarka and donated to MacBride Museum. Peter Clibbon's document, "The Evolution and Present Land Use Patterns of Whitehorse" and Paul Koroscil's article, "The Historical Development of Whitehorse, 1898-1945" are useful general histories of Whitehorse. The writings of Jim Lotz and Tim and Glenda Wilhelm offered much insight into the squatter situation from the late 1950s to the early 1970s.

A number of people were kind enough to share their memories of the waterfront in earlier days. John Scott gave us a vivid description of the shipyards in the 1920s and 1930s. Marvin Taylor, president and chief operating officer of White Pass Transportation Ltd., took time to talk about waterfront activity from 1942 on. Babe Richards shared interesting stories about the Pat Burns operation on the waterfront. Shipyards residents, Don and Sophie Miller and John Hatch, provided information about structures in the area.

Several repositories were consulted during our research. Judy Linton introduced us to the closet library at City Planning. Joanne Meehan, director and curator of MacBride Museum, offered access to the museum's research files and photograph collection. Stan Selmor, manager of Skagway Operations, offered the hospitality of the White Pass office in Skagway, while Suzanne Burnham and Anita Haskin helped with the hunt through the White Pass corporate records. As always, the staff of Yukon Archives were extremely helpful. Jim Robb and the Whitehorse Star contributed photographs.

Peter Thompson steered us to some useful waterfront plans. We were also assisted in tracing land ownership by Diane Gau and the able staff at the Land Titles Office, Mabel Macyshen at Federal Lands, Elsie Elrose at Territorial Lands, and Ken Steele at White Pass. Julie Cruikshank and Louise Profeit-LeBlanc kindly offered advice. Ella LeGresley shared historical information acquired during a separate study of the Shipyards area. Marjorie Copp of the Yukon Historical & Museums Association provided information from YHMA files. David Neufeld, our project manager, offered many useful suggestions, and generally was a pleasure to work with. Any errors in this work are solely our responsibility.

Our sincerest thanks to you all.

*Helene Dobrowolsky & Rob Ingram, Whitehorse 1994*

***Early view of the shipyards by moonlight, no date.***
*Yukon Archives / Maggie's Museum Collection*

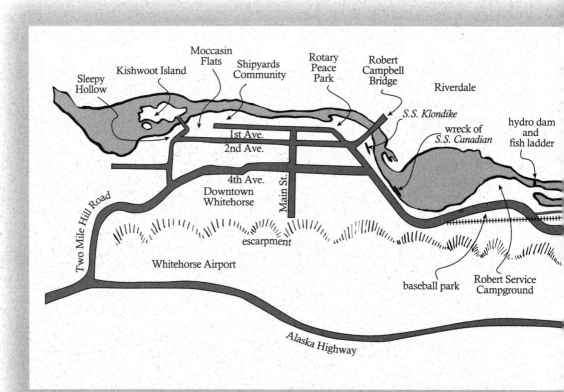

# THE WHITEHORSE WATERFRONT

Schwatka Lake

Canyon City

Miles Canyon

Robert Lowe
Foot Bridge

WP and Y Railway

Miles Canyon Road

South Access Road

#  PREFACE

**W**hitehorse is a water town. It was built to take advantage of the Yukon River as a transportation corridor. The railyards, shipyards, train crew's houses and squatters' shacks represent the forces that founded and built this city. This is what Whitehorse was before the flowering of the orderly subdivisions on the hills. Although the community has turned inland to the Alaska Highway, the river remains a central, if sometimes overlooked, element of our city's identity.

This is the second edition of *Edge of the River, Heart of the City*. The focus of this history is the period from 1898 to 1955. The first version was a background paper for waterfront planners as well as a history. The Yukon Historical & Museums Association, concerned that the city's waterfront heritage and identity were being forgotten, initiated historical research of the Whitehorse waterfront. By highlighting the area's heritage significance, the report encouraged decision-makers to consider the city's vital past in planning the new shape of the waterfront.

In this edition, we have tried to give the story more appeal to the general reader. The Yukon Historical & Museums Association hopes you will enjoy this book. Take it along for a walk on the edge of the river to appreciate this colourful and vital aspect of Whitehorse's history.

# EDGE OF THE RIVER
## HEART OF THE CITY

T he turbulent rapids were a good place to fish. They were also dangerous for anyone travelling by water—a place to unload a boat or raft and portage to safer, calmer waters. For thousands of years, Yukon's First Nations people met, fished, hunted and travelled this section of the Yukon River near present-day Whitehorse. It was part of their seasonal round of hunting and fishing. The frothing rapids that made this a portage point for original peoples also halted the newcomers in their northward journeys.

The first outsiders visiting the Yukon in the mid 19th century used the Yukon River and its tributaries as their major routes through the country. Once gold was discovered in the Klondike, these rivers became highways. While most mineral deposits were on creeks, the new settlements were usually some distance away on the major rivers and lakes at sites suitable for steamer landings. Town waterfronts were the focus of the community. Riverside lots were prime property—sought after for warehouses, stores, sawmills, residences and transport facilities. The

predominance of road and air transport after World War II changed all this. After the sternwheelers stopped running, the towns turned their backs on the water.

When thousands of goldseekers flooded into the territory during the Klondike Gold Rush of 1898, the riverbank below two major navigational hazards, Miles Canyon and White Horse Rapids, was transformed into the head of navigation on the Yukon River. It was a natural distribution point and logical settlement site. The builders of the White Pass and Yukon Railway decided that the flat on the west bank of the river was an ideal location for the railway terminus, and there they surveyed a townsite.

The town grew rapidly. Its heart was the river—the link between the world outside and the Yukon's political and economic centre, Dawson City. The railway followed the river into town, ran beside the warehouses and docks and continued on into the shipyards. Here the British Yukon Navigation Company (BYNCo.) built and maintained the fleet of steamers that serviced the Yukon River communities. The railway also served a number of other businesses along the waterfront. The stores, hotels, and government offices of Whitehorse grew in a triangular pattern from the waterfront with Front Street, later First Avenue, as the base and the top of Main Street as the apex.[1]

The primary forces which shaped the city emerged on the waterfront. White Pass instigated this development by bringing in the rail, then building the docks for the sternwheelers. The company built facilities for its rail terminal, and constructed boat building and maintenance shops.

Other business grew up around them, like the general merchants, Taylor & Drury, and the meat supplier, P. Burns & Company. People working in those industries, particularly on the trains and ships, built dwellings on the waterfront. This was also a cheap place to live, so transient workers and people who came to town seasonally often formed part of the community along the river.

The federal government held the 100-foot reserve and granted leases for use of the property. It held a certain balance of power by determining who would be granted waterfront leases and the terms of their tenure.

During the construction of the Alaska Highway and the accompanying invasion of military personnel and construction workers, the existing waterfront operations made Whitehorse a key distribution point. The railway and riverboats handled record loads of passengers and supplies. Several private and military float plane docks were moored along the riverbank. The great demand for housing during the war led to the mushroom growth of the squatter communities along the waterfront: Whiskey Flats, Moccasin Flats and Sleepy Hollow.

The Alaska Highway and postwar construction of all-weather roads to Dawson, Mayo and eventually, Skagway, reoriented the community away from the waterfront. Road and air travel supplanted rail and water, as the town turned inland to the Alaska Highway as its main connection with the Outside. The last of the sternwheelers stopped running in 1955. The end of railway freight and passenger service in 1982 completed this commercial severance from the riverfront.

In prosperous postwar Whitehorse, the thriving squatter communities on the waterfront became an embarrassment. The shacks of Whiskey Flats contrasted sharply with the posh new suburb of Riverdale across the river and were an affront to the taxpayers crossing the Robert Campbell Bridge. Whitehorse city administrators wished to take a more orderly approach to city planning. The eccentric, independent communities along the waterfront had no place in this vision. They could not be easily wished away, however, and the next 35 years saw many approaches and confrontations in an ongoing attempt to resolve the squatter "problem."

In the late 1960s, Whitehorse began to look on its waterfront as a potential resource, an attractive site for recreational and commercial activity. Whiskey Flats became a park and the new resting place of the *S.S. Klondike*, now a National Historic Site. Over the next two decades, many waterfront plans were prepared but to date there has been little development.

With the waterfront on the verge of change once again, it is time to pause and reflect on a piece of our forgotten history—the busy and vital past of the edge of the river.

# THE EARLY DAYS

## ⇒ FIRST NATIONS ⇐

Preliminary archaeological surveys of the banks of the Yukon River north from Miles Canyon show signs of cultural occupation well before the contact period. The area around Whitehorse was once an extended range for woodland bison which were hunted by First Nations people.[2] It is also known that seasonal fishing camps were located above and below Miles Canyon.[3] Frederick Schwatka's expedition down the Yukon River in 1883 used an Aboriginal portage trail on the east bank of the river. The "Takheesh" man who guided Schwatka's group to the portage site navigated the river in a dug-out cottonwood canoe.[4]

Although First Nations people did use rafts and canoes, most preferred to travel on foot trails. Since the first Euro-Americans tended to use the rivers as their main highways, there were few encounters with the indigenous population. Consequently, many visitors reported that the Aboriginal population was small.[5]

This stretch of the river and its fishing sites were important to a number of First Nations. Yukon Aboriginal people travelled widely during their yearly cycle of fishing, hunting and trapping. There were no clear-cut boundaries defining areas of use and it is likely that the portage trail around Miles Canyon was variously used by Southern Tutchone, Tagish and Tlingit First Nations.

After the great influx of newcomers during the Klondike Gold Rush, First Nations people continued to make the Whitehorse area part of their seasonal round. Living in camps and simple dwellings on the edges of town, they used Whitehorse as a base for trading, trapping, and seasonal jobs on the boats and at wood camps.

The coming of the Alaska Highway brought yet more change to the lives of Yukon Aboriginal people. For many it meant the end of a traditional lifestyle and moving closer to towns to take advantage of schools and jobs. In Whitehorse, many settled in the riverbank communities and were subsequently affected by the postwar squatter evictions and relocations.

It is important to recognize the role of First Nations people in any examination of waterfront history. We hope that future archaeology and oral history work will add more to the story of the first peoples' lives along the river.

# MILES CANYON

There were few practical routes to the Klondike goldfields. The most-travelled extended from Skagway, over the mountain passes to the headwater lakes, then down the Yukon River to Dawson City. While the route was popular, it was far from smooth.

The treacherous six mile stretch of water formed by Miles Canyon and the White Horse Rapids was all but impassable. Schwatka, on his 1883 expedition for the U.S. Army, wrote a vivid description of the canyon and the rapids:

*Through this narrow chute of corrugated rock the wild waters of the great river rush in a perfect mass of milk-like foam, with a reverberation that is audible for a considerable distance, the roar being intensified by the rocky walls which act like so many sounding*

**Shooting Miles Canyon with empty scow at high water, 1899.**
*Yukon Archives / Forrest Collection*

*boards.…At the northern outlet of the cañon, the river spreads rapidly into its former width, but abates not a jot of its swiftness, and flows in a white and shallow sheet over reefs of bowlders* [sic] *and bars thickly studded with intertwining drifts of huge timber, ten times more dangerous for a boat or a raft than the narrow cañon itself.…*[6]

The Southern Tutchone people in the area called the canyon, Kwänlin, meaning "water running through canyon."[7] Early prospectors referred to the canyon as the "Grand Canyon." In 1883, Schwatka renamed it Miles Canyon after his superior officer, Brigadier General Nelson A. Miles. While there are a number of fanciful stories for how the White Horse Rapids were named, the most likely seems to be that the foaming white waters reminded early visitors of the manes of white horses.[8]

When a hydro dam was constructed below the rapids in 1958, the canyon waters rose and the rapids disappeared under what became known as Schwatka Lake.

***Steamers Gleaner, Australian and Nora docked at Canyon City, ca. 1898.***
*Yukon Archives 2695 / Hegg Collection*

Although the wild waters have been tamed, historic photographs remain to evoke the dangers of navigating the rapids.

Steamers plying the Yukon River were forced to halt at either end of the rapids and wait for goods and passengers to make their way past the hazard. Most stampeders chose to transport their goods around the dangerous water along the portage trail on the east bank. By 1898, they were able to use Norman Macaulay's tramline, the Canyon and White Horse Rapids Tramway Company, consisting of horse-drawn carts on log rails. The roadhouse, barns and associated structures at the upriver end of the tramway became known as Canyon City. The small tent community that arose at the tramline terminus, today the site of Riverdale, became known as White Horse.

Macauley's business thrived after North West Mounted Police Superintendent Sam Steele ruled that only experienced pilots could steer empty boats through the dangerous rapids. Passengers and goods would have to travel overland. John Hepburn briefly operated another tramline on the west bank of the river before Macaulay bought him out in June 1899 to gain complete control of passage around this bottleneck.

*Tents, horse-drawn tramline cars and sternwheelers docked along the east bank of the Yukon River at the original townsite of White Horse, July 1899.*
Yukon Archives 1337/University of Washington Collection

Soon, Macaulay himself gave way to more powerful interests. The White Pass and Yukon Railway was also interested in capitalizing on the stampede of Klondike prospectors. Later, in 1899, it bought out the tramways to eliminate competition and insure unimpeded access to the head of navigation on the Yukon River.[9]

# THE FOUNDING OF WHITEHORSE

The railway owners were not just interested in running a railway. They planned a transportation system connecting tidewater at Skagway to the Klondike goldfields. Although the builders had originally planned to continue the railway on to Fort Selkirk, the expense and the established system of steamers at White Horse caused them to reconsider. White Horse was to remain the end of steel.

In October 1899, the company commissioned the survey of a new townsite on the west bank of the river. It decided to christen the new settlement Closeleigh, after Close Brothers & Company of London, major financiers of the railway. The Yukon's commissioner, William Ogilvie, decided otherwise. In late 1899, he requested that a post office under the name of White Horse (in later years shortened to Whitehorse) be established at the new townsite.[10]

By the time the railway came into town on June 8th, 1900, the river flat was occupied by a rapidly-growing tent community, soon to become the Yukon's principal distribution centre.

## THE COMPANY TOWN

The White Pass & Yukon Route Limited (WP&YR) was to influence and, to a large extent, control the fortunes of Whitehorse for the next 50 years. After the original survey, the company employed a number of agents to buy most of the property in the new townsite for $34,000, thus gaining control over most subsequent land transactions in Whitehorse.

The White Pass & Yukon Route Limited was a multifaceted operation. Subsidiary companies were created to handle the various aspects of its business. One of these, the British Yukon Mining, Trading & Transportation Company (later the British Yukon Railway Company), obtained a concession of 97.12 acres for rail yards, an area covering the entire southern end of the townsite flat, as well as land for the railway right of way. Its land division, the British Yukon Land Company Limited, handled land transactions in the Yukon including lot purchases and sales in the new community of Whitehorse. The town was laid out in 17 large lots, four of which were subdivided into smaller building lots. Most of these were sold or leased to private individuals. One-third of the townsite was set aside for federal government use, as required by law.

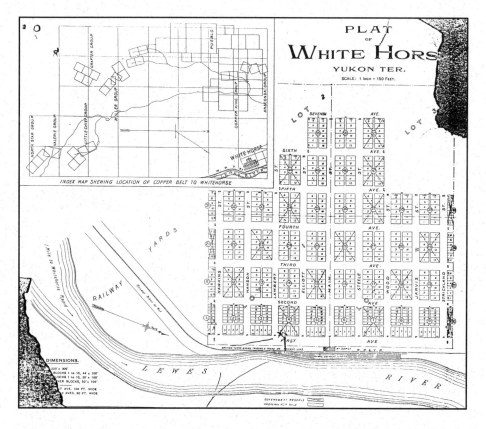

*Plat of White Horse, ca. 1900. Up until 1945, the section of the Yukon River above the Pelly River was officially known as the Lewes River.*
Yukon Archives / YRG I, Series 1, vol. 13, f. 2788

The company reserved most of the riverfront property for its own operations: the railway right of way, railway yards, docks, the depot building, warehouses and a shipyard. This was obtained by land purchase and a series of riverfront leases from the federal government. The leases permitted the use of land within the crown reserve, the 100-foot strip extending inland from the ordinary high water mark. Today, White Pass still owns much land along the waterfront as well as various other properties in Whitehorse. Indeed, it was not until the 1950s, that ownership of the streets was transferred from White Pass to the city.[11]

While by today's standards this seems like an enormous amount of land for one private agency to control, Whitehorse was basically a one industry town. Even the copper mining activities in the hills west of town owed their sporadic prosperity to the existence of the railway's connection to tidewater and the smelters of the south. Whitehorse existed because it was the head of river navigation and the end of

steel, a transshipment and distribution point. White Pass & Yukon Route Limited made that possible and the company provided the focus of the town's economy.

## Early Whitehorse and the Waterfront

The buildings, railway, docks, and vessels along the waterfront dominate a panorama of Whitehorse, photographed in September 1900. The new track runs along the river bank to the docks on the north. The many small boats tied up along the shore contrast with the large steamer docked further downstream. The mélange of structures range from tents and small cabins to two-storey log commercial buildings with boom town fronts. The most imposing edifices, however, are the new White Pass railway depot and warehouses on the riverside docks. Almost all

*Panorama of Whitehorse, September 1900.* Yukon Archives 4070/MacBride Museum Collection

buildings are oriented toward the railway and the river. This was the face that Whitehorse showed to the world at the turn of the century.

Over the winter of 1900 and throughout the following year, buildings and businesses moved to the new town from the short-lived settlement across the river and from the rapidly dwindling townsite of Bennett, British Columbia, at the end of the gold rush trails. One of the first buildings to appear on Front Street (now First Avenue) was a log structure called the Closeleigh Hotel and Saloon. Two portions of this building still exist in Moccasin Flats as cabins.

Glowing newspaper accounts of the time listed each new business in town almost as soon as it erected a tent or began raising logs. From the outset, newspaper stories were quick to remark on the significance of the townsite as a terminal for both the railway and the steamboat lines. Much excitement was expressed concerning the potential wealth generated by the copper discoveries. One writer cheerfully suggested that "next summer will see not less than 8000 people in Closeleigh."[12] This prediction proved overly optimistic but the summer did bring rapid expansion. While reading an account of construction activities in May, one can almost hear the pounding hammers and smell the sawdust:

> *The population of White Horse, according to the census taken by the N.W.M.P. [North West Mounted Police] a few weeks ago, is about 250, and from present indications will double that number by the time navigation opens...Building and improvements will now proceed rapidly. The following named firms are now doing business: Closeleigh hotel and saloon, Smart & Dixon proprietors; Regina hotel, J.C. Johnson, proprietor; Bartlett hotel and saloon, Bartlett Brothers, proprietors; Canadian Bank of Commerce, H.M. Lay, manager; Whitney and Pedlar, general merchandise and meats; C. Chambers, newspapers and magazines. The British American Corporation are erecting a two story [sic] frame building for hotel and saloon purposes. Racine & Dixon are getting out logs for a 26 x 60 building in which they will operate a steam laundry and planing mill, and a number of new enterprises are expected in the near future.[13]*

The pace never slowed over the summer. When the photographer H.C. Barley visited Whitehorse in late June, he pronounced the scene "a regular old time boom." Hotels were full and many were sleeping on the steamboats, while the gambling houses were "running wide open." The post office opened on July 1st, 1900. Whitehorse became an official port of entry with the opening of a customs office on August 20th. Two newspapers set up offices, the *White Horse Tribune* and the *White Horse Star.* By the time Governor General Lord Minto made his grand tour to the Klondike in late summer, the members of the newly-organized Board of Trade were on hand to welcome His Excellency to town. Land speculation was rampant and by late November, a town lot in a prime location was changing hands for as much as $3,000.[14]

The official opening of the railway at Carcross on July 29th, 1900 was an occasion of great celebration and optimism. The railway's general manager, E.C. Hawkins, made much of the new White Pass riverfront facilities in Whitehorse:

*We have completed the best possible facilities for handling perishables at Whitehorse...and are in a position to handle goods with the least possible delay, and greatest care. A wharf, the best on the river, 800 feet long, has been built, and on it a warehouse 40 x 600 feet, which will accommodate about 3000 tons of freight. Three tracks are laid on the wharf and cars coming in loaded are run right down to the steamer's side, and the freight transferred direct from car to steamer, which arrangement possesses great advantages over the old way.[15]*

In under two years, Whitehorse had grown from a place at the foot of the rapids to a bustling community with a burgeoning transportation industry. The White Pass & Yukon Route was the driving force behind this creation. But other entrepreneurs and interests were beginning to blossom along the riverbank. These independents lent diversity and colour to the waterfront and the town, otherwise overpoweringly White Pass. The company had not finished building on the riverbank, however. A whole new dimension was being added to its enterprises.

**Scow full of lumber running White Horse Rapids, ca. 1898.**
*Yukon Archives / Hamacher Collection*

# *THE RIVER DIVISION:*
# THE BRITISH YUKON NAVIGATION COMPANY

Until the Klondike Gold Rush, the main water route into the Yukon interior was via the lower Yukon River, from the coast at St. Michael, Alaska. The introduction of steamer traffic on the upper Yukon River in 1898, followed by the completion of the railway two years later, made the upper river route from Whitehorse to Dawson the primary gateway to the Yukon's interior. By the time the railway opened, gold rush excitement was ebbing, and many of the transportation companies that had plied the river in 1898 were closing down.

*The newly-built sternwheelers Whitehorse, Dawson and Selkirk with workers posing on all decks, May 25, 1901. Construction was completed 43 days after the keels were laid.*
*Yukon Archives 5550/Barley Collection*

White Pass decided to establish its own river service. Difficulties arising from the transfer of goods to unreliable shipping companies had led to a number of claims being levied against the railroad company. But mainly, company officials realized ownership of the railway would almost guarantee a monopoly on upper river traffic. The river arm of White Pass, the British Yukon Navigation Company (BYNCo.), was formed over the winter of 1900–1901. The company set up a shipyard in Whitehorse, downstream from the docks and warehouses, and began building its own steamers.

On May 1st, 1901, the BYNCo. bought the assets of the Canadian Development Company. Two years later all but three steamers on the upper river were owned by the BYNCo. While the White Pass River Division now controlled the upper river, the various steamship companies fought for control of the lower river traffic between St. Michael and Dawson City. In 1913, the BYNCo. launched two new steamers from the Whitehorse shipyards, *Alaska* and *Yukon,* built expressly for lower river traffic. After fierce tariff wars, the BYNCo. emerged the winner in 1914. It bought out its chief rival on the lower river, the Northern Commercial Company. Its service was complemented by smaller companies freighting on the shallower side streams such as the Stewart, Fortymile and Pelly rivers.

The Canadian government intervened to open up these lesser waterways in the first decade of the century, offering free transportation to prospectors willing to explore new mining country. The White Pass gained control of the Stewart River trade by developing a system for transshipping ore from Mayo to its ships on the Yukon River. By the mid 1920s, however, the River Division was greatly reduced in size. The opening of the Alaska Railroad between Valdez and Fairbanks in 1922 curtailed the lower river operation. The onset of the depression placed additional strain on the White Pass River Division.[16]

The White Pass & Yukon Route was now a major player in the territory's economic fortunes. The company's well-being depended upon the Yukon's prosperity. Conversely, as a major employer and the main carrier to the Outside, the company could influence the territorial economy through lay-offs and high tariff rates. Consequently, the fortunes of White Pass dictated the level of economic activity along the waterfront and affected the prosperity of Whitehorse.

# SQUABBLES & SQUATTERS

In April 1901, the company requested an additional 800-foot lease to permit access to its shipyards. The new lease would have extended immediately downriver of the existing 1,500-foot White Pass lease.

When White Pass made its application, the company's lawyers stated that the river frontage was needed for launching and hauling out boats and, *so as to prevent squatters from erecting shanties or making other use of the water front which would interfere with the free use of it by the Navigation Company for the purpose of their business.*[17]

The local Board of Trade took great exception to the application. It claimed White Pass would monopolize the waterfront, not only shutting out other businesses with prior applications, but blocking community access to the river as well. Eventually, the lease was granted but revised to commence further downriver, from the north end of Strickland Street.

The area between the two White Pass waterfront leases was occupied by the White Horse Steam Laundry and the Yukon Electric Works Ltd. Areas were also set aside for the Department of Public Works and the North West Mounted Police. The public was given river access through an 80-foot stretch of waterfront. Other tenants referred to in early government records were R. W. Calderhead and Robert Kelly, but there is no mention of the nature of their businesses. The lumber dealer, Upper Yukon Consolidated Company, for a time worked out of what became the shipyards area. When Taylor & Drury started to set up branch stores at various river settlements, the company docked its boat in this area as well.

This was the first mention of an oft-repeated theme over the next 90 years. During boom times the community welcomed an influx of much-needed workers, despite lacking sufficient accommodation or services to handle the sudden increases in population. The usual solution adopted by the overflow populace was to construct simple dwellings on the outskirts of town. The squatter structures were generally ignored by land owners, usually White Pass or the Crown, until the land was required for other purposes. According to White Pass, 400 to 500 shipyard workers were working in the shipyards in May 1900. It is likely that many of these seasonal workers chose to erect simple dwellings near their place of work.

The squatters are mentioned again in a company file of 1908–09. The company's general manager wrote an interesting letter to the auditor regarding the shacks built by longshore crew and others on vacant company lots in the townsite:

*I think these shacks should be removed, and would request you to take this up with Mr. Phelps, and go through the necessary motions so that we can have them destroyed without incurring any liability.*

*Regarding Mr. McLennan's attempt to assess us $110.00 for houses in "chippy town," I understand that lots are assessable only in a recorded townsite, and as the White Horse "red light district" is outside of the townsite, there is no earthly reason why we should pay this tax.*

Attempts to remove the dwellings were unsuccessful. The company's Whitehorse lawyer, W.L. Phelps, instead offered the tenants a lease agreement, charging rental of $12 per year. There is no record of any efforts to either evict or sign lease agreements with the "sporting houses" in the red light district north of town, also referred to as "Prestonville" in a later communication.[18]

The waterfront was used by transients as well as long-term residents. Transient is perhaps a misnomer, however, since it was often the same people who returned to live on the waterfront every year. Shipyard and boat crews were seasonal workers. Many shipyard workers lived here while they were in the north and many of the boat crews stayed here only when their boats were in town.

Aboriginal peoples lived along the riverside as well. When in town for supplies, or hunting or trapping in the area, people tented or stayed in the small shacks and houses along the river. It was cheap and tenancy was informal. First Nations people also worked on the boats during the summer and cut wood or trapped during the winter months. For the time that they were working on the vessels, some lived near the shipyards. One of these was the famous riverboat pilot, Frank Slim. His daughter, Sophie Miller, still lives in the Shipyards area.

While it may be a contradiction to say a stable squatter community emerged, it is obvious the squatters were a constant presence on the waterfront from early in the city's history.

# THE WATERFRONT HEYDAY

WHITEHORSE Y.T. photo taken at midnight.

*View of the Whitehorse shipyards looking southwest, no date. The set of ways in the foreground was known as the "boneyard," and used to store ships out of service.*
*Yukon Archives/Galigan Collection*

## ⊹⟶ THE SHIPYARDS: ⟵⊹ THE YEARLY ROUND

When people think of Whitehorse as a company town, the railway usually springs to mind. This was not so, however. Most industry generated by the railway, such as the shops to build new rolling stock, was based in Skagway. The majority of people working on the railway were Skagway residents. Although the railway brought Whitehorse into existence, it was the British Yukon Navigation Company and its shipyard operations that kept the town going.[19]

In 1922 Whitehorse had a year-round population of about 350. There were few permanent jobs and the town tended to shut down in October at the close of navigation. In late March, the boat crews began coming back to town on the train. For many residents, a sure sign of spring was the blast of the steam whistle in the shipyards which summoned the crews to work.

About 60 people worked in the shipyards before spring break-up opened the river. The first arrivals, the steamboat engineers and firemen, worked on the ships' engines and boilers. The bull gang cleared ice and snow from the ways and around the hulls, allowing the ship carpenters to make repairs. Routine maintenance of the hulls included replacing damaged planking, caulking gaps, tarring and repainting. John Scott, who moved to Whitehorse at the age of 11 in 1922, fondly remembers rainy days when the carpenters sat in the hull of the abandoned steamer, *Bonanza King*, gossiping as they rolled oakum into long ropes for caulking.

*Sternwheelers Selkirk, Dawson and Whitehorse at Whitehorse shipyards, ca. 1904.*
British Columbia Archives 20073

The most striking feature of the shipyards at this time of year was the sight of the BYNCo. fleet blocked up on the three sets of ways. These sloping ramps were used for launching the boats in the spring and hauling them out of the water in the fall. Closer examination of the area, however, reveals a number of buildings behind the boats. Although these structures did not look very imposing, they represented a complete shipbuilding facility. The complex of buildings included a tinsmith's shop, steam chests for bending planks, a planing mill, a paint shop, boiler house, coal bin, engine repair shop, bunk houses and mess hall. For the town's youth, the most fascinating place was the blacksmith's shop. They spent hours watching the blacksmith fashion a variety of intricate metal parts from bar iron and iron plate.

Many of the famous steamers that plied the Yukon River were built in the Whitehorse shipyards. The *Alaska* (later renamed *Aksala*) and the *Yukon* were built

*Launching of the sternwheeler Casca, ca. 1942.*
Yukon Archives 8288 / Tidd Collection

for lower river traffic. The *Whitehorse* and the *Casca* handled the tourist trade. The *Keno* was designed for the Stewart River, to freight ore downstream from Mayo to the confluence of the Stewart and Yukon rivers, at Stewart Island. The main function of the first and second *Klondike* was transporting silver-lead ore up the Yukon River from Stewart Island to Whitehorse.

As soon as the river ice was out, the boats were launched—an arduous and labour-intensive process. Using about 20 large screw jacks, the bull gang gradually lowered the boats onto greased "butterboards," or skids, to slide down the ways into the water.

Once the sternwheelers were afloat, the activity moved upriver to the complex of docks, offices, and warehouses clustered around the train depot. The dock area was a busy and efficient transshipment point between the railway and the steamers.

*River warehouse and dock looking north, 1901. Note the large freight doors and slips.*
Yukon Archives 5548 / Barley Collection

Freight was offloaded from the trains directly into the river warehouse. Several large freight doors with slips or ramps gave directly onto the dock, allowing a number of steamers to be loaded simultaneously. The longshore crew moved most freight by hand, but a large steam-driven derrick handled heavy items such as Dawson-bound dredge equipment. The river warehouse also featured a four-hole privy hanging over the river. A local pastime was fishing through the privy holes, usually a source of fat grayling.

Inland from the river warehouse, across the tracks, was the local warehouse. This building stored freight destined for Whitehorse and for other southern communities reached by overland travel. Upriver, at the south end of the depot, was the commissary. This housed a few offices, food and supplies for the riverboats and railway section houses, and supplies for the longshore gang including a coal bin to fuel the steam derrick. Upstairs, in the dormered area, were bedrooms for single employees. An ice house, south of the commissary, stored large blocks of ice buried in sawdust. The ice was used on the riverboats to refrigerate perishable foods.

The docks were also a focus for people. With the opening of the railway, the WP&YR published a number of tourism pamphlets highlighting the glories of the northern countryside and its colourful Klondike Gold Rush history. The railway

*Whitehorse waterfront ca. 1912.*
*View of ice house (left) and commissary (foreground).*
Yukon Archives 4103 / MacBride Museum Collection

and river divisions collaborated with the coastal steamship lines to offer tours. These tourist ventures were tightly scheduled to meet the various boat and train timetables. Those fortunate enough to take a sternwheeler excursion marvelled at the splendid scenery, gourmet meals, excellent service and fine appointments.

In summer, the depot and docks were easily the most exciting place in town. Residents often strolled out to meet the train or boat. Receptions for local dignitaries took place right on the docks.

Three months later, however, the same site would be virtually abandoned—the river frozen, the steamers back on the ways, most of the shipyard and boat crews gone south for the winter, and only one or two trains a week coming into the depot.

## SO WHO ELSE USED THE WATERFRONT?

While they were very close to having dominion over the waterfront, the railway and BYNCo. did not have a complete monopoly. From the founding of the town

*Whitehorse residents throng on the dock to welcome Earl Grey, Governor General of Canada, August 10, 1909.*
Yukon Archives 4103/MacBride Museum Collection

until the late 1930s, the waterfront was a hive of activity for a wide range of other occupants. Although the town was concentrated between Hawkins and Strickland streets, the waterfront was in use the full length of the river flat.

There were several reasons why the waterfront drew such a great number and variety of tenants. The attraction to the waterfront for businesses was, of course, the dependence on water, whether it was required for transportation or as part of the mechanics of the operation, such as a laundry. For those living by the river, proximity to the water and its associated industries was important, but it also meant cheap living quarters close to town. For seasonal and out-of-town workers, it was much more feasible to build or rent a small, cheap place on land one did not have to buy. Ship and train workers fell into this category of inhabitant as did First Nations people. For Aboriginal people, used to a subsistence lifestyle which kept them on the move, permanent dwellings with fixed costs made little sense.

The occupants of the waterfront were hardly a homogeneous lot. Yet even this diverse group, the squatters and the railway, the laundry and lumberyards, the shipyards and stockyards all held something in common—their reliance upon the water. To a certain degree they were also dependent on each other. Even the mighty BYNCo. needed its deckhands.

At the extreme south end, where the railway entered Whitehorse along the escarpment, were railway structures. The Wye area contained the train shed or roundhouse, engine crew's bunkhouse, hostler's cabin, pump house and coal

*Early view of the south end of Whitehorse showing the trainyards, ca. 1904.*
*British Columbia Archives 20228*

bunkers. For a short period, there was a stockyard as well. Further along the line, just before the railway entered town, stood a section house and tool shed. The only extant remnant of these railway structures is the Casey House. This small building housed the motor car or casey car used by section crews to patrol the tracks and make repairs (see map page 57).

Train crew members, mostly Skagway residents, built small dwellings for use during their Whitehorse layovers, which could last up to ten days in winter. These diminutive dwellings were built on the west side of the tracks.[20] Although technically squatting on White Pass land their presence was tolerated by the company.[21]

The area later known as North Whiskey Flats, now Rotary Peace Park, was also occupied. An early resident, Shorty Roils, owned a cabin, garden and greenhouse. He worked on the longshore gang and, as a sideline, sold vegetables in town.[22]

The area was also home to some First Nations people. The late First Nations Elder, Angela Sidney, stayed on the waterfront intermittently in 1914-15 when she was a girl; her family was hunting foxes in the Whitehorse area. She mentioned that a number of other families were living there at the time.[23]

Near the present site of the Yukon government building, the Millhaven Lumber Company held a lease.

Further downriver, between Hanson and Elliot Streets, there were a number of little buildings. These were probably dwellings of longshore workers, including the residence of the dock foreman just north of the ice house. The two small buildings still on site are of a later vintage but it is likely that they were built for the same purpose. Apparently, the most southerly building was constructed in the early 1950s to house the White Pass watchman and his wife.[24] Until recently, a longtime train worker lived in the other.

*The WP&YR train station and the Fire Hall, November 1901.*
Yukon Archives 605/PAC Collection

# Fire Hall/Yukon Electrical Co. Building

In 1901, the Fire Hall was built south of the railway station. Its strategic location in the downtown core proved of little use on May 23rd, 1905. Fire broke out in the barbershop at the rear of the Windsor Hotel. The pump and water supply failed and the fire raged along Front Street for two blocks, destroying buildings to a value of nearly $300,000. The casualties included the White Pass depot, some wharf buildings, and five hotels.[25]

After the fire, the Yukon Electrical Company made an agreement to move next to the Fire Hall and service the boilers and pumps necessary to operate the fire equipment. The YEC building was joined to the south side of the Fire Hall and both still stand on the site today.

# Railway Depot

When the WP&YR built the railway station and dock complex in 1900, one local business owner boasted: *the WP&YR have a depot and warehouse at White Horse that would be a credit to a town the size of Seattle.*[26] Indeed, in a fledgling town that still featured tents and simple log buildings as the main type of architecture, the station

*Waterfront view of the White Pass & Yukon Railway depot before the 1905 fire, June 1901.*
*Yukon Archives 5556/Barley Collection*

26

stood in sharp contrast as a handsome and substantial framed edifice. It anchored one end of Main Street and became a focus for the town, a function it still serves today.

The original building was destroyed in the 1905 fire but was quickly rebuilt using a similar design. The building remained essentially unchanged until major alterations were made during World War II.

On the river side of the station were extensive wharfage and warehousing. To the north, the land was mostly given over to rail yards up to the boat building and dry-dock area.

## REDDICK'S BOAT BUILDING

This was a one-man boat building company on the banks of the Yukon River opposite the Regina Hotel. For many years Bob Reddick sold rowboats for about $25 to people travelling downstream to Dawson, a cheaper alternative to an expensive sternwheeler fare.[27]

*Mrs. Sharp, her son and an elderly man*
*at the site of Reddick's boat-building operation, no date.*
Yukon Archives 6183 / Harbottle Collection

# TAYLOR & DRURY DOCKING AREA

The Taylor & Drury Company had its docking area at the foot of Strickland Street, not far from its main store on the corner of Front (now First Avenue) and Main streets.

Taylor & Drury and its branch stores occupied an important niche in the Yukon's economy. Most of its 16 or so trading posts were situated on tributary rivers of the Yukon River, areas not serviced by White Pass. By setting up trading posts in remote communities, Taylor & Drury fostered the Yukon's fur trade.

A small set of ways served as the winter resting place for the T&D boat. Three different vessels occupied this site over the years: the *Kluane*, the *Thistle* and the *Yukon Rose*. The steamer *Kluane* was built on this site about 1905, using engines from England. As T&D operations expanded, the *Kluane* had difficulty servicing their many branch posts. In 1919, the company bought the *Thistle*, a BYNCo. steamer that was being withdrawn from river service. The *Thistle* plied the Yukon side streams for ten years until she sank during a storm on Lake Laberge. The *Yukon Rose*, a propeller-driven tunnel boat, was the *Thistle's* successor and served the company until World War II.[28]

# WHITE HORSE STEAM LAUNDRY

*White Horse Steam Laundry wagon on Main Street, no date.*
Yukon Archives 4104/MacBride Museum Collection

This enterprise was founded by early Whitehorse entrepreneur, Ed Dixon. Shortly after selling out his interest in the Pioneer Hotel, Mr. Dixon built and operated a small laundry. In 1901, this building was replaced by the White Horse Laundry, a 40 x 60 foot log building housing a steam laundry plant. This imposing structure dominated the waterfront for many years. Apparently, the laundry also housed the beginnings of the town's electrical supply:

*Mr. Dixon has recently added to the modern conveniences of his plant by putting in electric light, having his own dynamo operated by power from the laundry engine. He also furnishes the current for lighting the White Horse Hotel and his plant may form a nucleus for a complete electric light system for the entire town within the near future.*[29]

As well as individual orders, the plant handled the laundry for the hotels and the White Pass steamers in the summer. Eventually, this structure was replaced by a dry-cleaning plant, with apartments. In its final years, it was a second-hand store. This building, locally known as the "20-20," contained some timbers of the original steam laundry. It was destroyed by fire in November 1985.[30]

## SHIPYARDS COMMUNITY

This section of waterfront extends from the shipyards downriver to Kishwoot Island. An undetermined portion of this area includes Moccasin Flats, probably christened during the great expansion of this squatter community during World War II.

Early in the century, one only had to travel a short distance north of town before Whitehorse took on a decidedly rural atmosphere. A long, skinny slough extended

*Section of waterfront looking north, ca. 1905. From the foreground back,*
*one can see a rowboat from a small boat-building business,*
*the T&D steamer Kluane on ways, the Whitehorse Steam Laundry,*
*the tall chimney of the Yukon Electrical Co. steam plant, and the vessels of the BYNCo.*
*Yukon Archives 4637/AHS Collection*

inland from a point opposite Kishwoot Island, parallelling the river south to the area behind the shipyards. West of the slough were two small ponds. Between the shipyards and the slough were the barn and other structures associated with the Whitehorse to Dawson Overland Trail. People living north and west of this area maintained rural establishments such as stables, ranches and fox farms.

In 1910, James D. Richards took out a 60-foot waterfront lease north of the shipyards to operate a sawmill. Richards ran into various business difficulties and was unable to meet his lease rental fees. The business closed down after about five years but Richards or "Buzzsaw Jimmy," as he was better known, continued cutting wood around town. He achieved renown as the inventor of a buzzsaw on wheels put together from an old tractor, a Model T Ford and various other iron scraps. The portable saw cut wood into stove lengths at the rate of eight to ten cords per hour.[31]

At the extreme northern limit of the waterfront was one of the town's less savoury businesses, the stockyards and slaughterhouse of P. Burns & Company. Pat Burns obtained this 350-foot lease about 1901. Live cattle and hogs were shipped into town by rail then butchered before being sold in the Whitehorse store on Main Street and elsewhere in the territory. The "slaughterhouse" was actually a tiny shed. Well-known Whitehorse entrepreneur T.C. Richards managed this operation from 1915 until it closed down around 1932. By that time, it was no longer necessary to ship meat on the hoof. Refrigerated storage facilities on the ships and trains made it possible to order precut, frozen carcasses.

The town dump was on the riverbank next to the Burns facility. Garbage was dumped on the bank and periodically pushed over into the river. It was not until the American Army took over this site in the early 1940s that the dump was moved further downstream to McIntyre Creek.[32]

A number of small dwellings, most belonging to shipyard carpenters, were also interspersed throughout this area. Early plans of the site show a number of tents as well as more solid structures. One small building which started out as a wall tent, was erected by John Sewell after he moved to Whitehorse in 1904. Fifteen years later, Mr. Sewell took over a general store on Front Street near the Regina Hotel and lived upstairs in the living quarters. Sewell's humble Shipyards building still stands and has housed many people over the years, including Louis Irvine, Henry Broeren, Alice and Lawrence Sam, and riverboat pilot, Frank Slim.[33]

# FRANK SLIM

Frank Slim was born at Marsh Lake in 1898. As a boy, he used to paddle to Canyon City by dugout canoe then walk the old tramway line into Whitehorse. In 1917, he married Agnes Broeren and they had a family of five children. He was a well-known riverboat pilot who worked on most major Yukon rivers—the Yukon, the Pelly, the Nisutlin and the Stewart. He also navigated the Dease and Stikine rivers in British Columbia as well as the Tanana in Alaska. Frank Slim piloted many boats, including the Taylor & Drury supply boat *Yukon Rose*, but his favourite was the *Klondike*. After the steamers stopped running, Slim ran river ferries, operated heavy equipment, trapped and bought fur. In 1964, he piloted the *Keno* on its last voyage from Whitehorse to Dawson. Mount Slim, southeast of Lake Laberge, was named in his memory shortly after his death in 1973.[34]

***Frank Slim stands by the paddlewheel of the beached steamer Casca, ca. early 1970s.***
*©Jim Robb photo*

# WINGS ON THE WATERFRONT

The late 1920s brought a newcomer to the northern transportation network, commercial aviation. During the pioneer period of Yukon air travel, there were few airstrips. The lakes and rivers, however, provided an abundance of landing sites for planes rigged with floats and skis.[35] Consequently, the Yukon River and the Whitehorse waterfront played an important role in the development of the Yukon's fledgling aviation industry.

By the late 1930s, Whitehorse residents had become accustomed to the sight and sound of airplanes landing on the water or ice of the Yukon River. The WP&YR, always quick to spot an opportunity, set up its Canadian air service in 1935. British Yukon Aviation (also called White Pass Airways) soon became the largest airline in the territory. Although White Pass built a hangar by the landing field on the escarpment above town, it also used the river, giving access to existing rail and

*WP&YR's first Ford tri-motor on the frozen Yukon River in front of the river shed on the Whitehorse waterfront, ca. 1935/36. Freight is being transferred to WP&YR's smaller Fairchild 82 airplane.* Yukon Archives 6072/Harbottle Collection

water facilities. Pan American Airways also used the waterfront in the 1930s, and had a dock near the north end of what is now Rotary Peace Park.[36]

In 1934, United Air Transport of Edmonton began chartered flights into the Yukon. Three years later the company obtained a waterfront lease for a plane base, downriver from Buzzsaw Jimmy's sawmill site. The company thrived despite active opposition from White Pass during its early days in the Yukon. On his first flight to the Yukon, Grant McConachie received the following warning from a local minister:

> *You must know, Mr. McConachie, that Whitehorse is a company town; Whitepass [sic] and Yukon owns it...You'll have trouble getting gas. They won't throw you a rope, tie you up at the dock or even give you the time of day.[37]*

In 1938, the company's assets were transferred to Yukon Southern Air Transport Ltd. It, in turn, became part of Canadian Pacific Airlines in 1942.[38]

# WARTIME—BOOM TIME

Little happened to change the pace of life in Whitehorse during the 1920s and 1930s. It remained a sleepy little town that woke up in the spring, bustled all summer, then settled back into winter hibernation. During the depression, people lived simply and got by. No one could guess that the bombing of a small tropical isle half the world away would change all that.

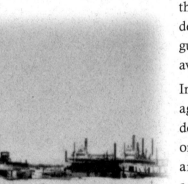

In early 1942, the American and Canadian governments agreed to construct a highway to Alaska as a wartime defence project. This decision was to have a profound effect on the entire Yukon, but it particularly affected Whitehorse and its residents. Whitehorse became an important administrative and distribution centre due to its strategic location at the end of steel, its recently modernized airport, and its water connections. From Whitehorse, construction equipment and supplies could be freighted to sites as divergent as Teslin and Circle, Alaska.[39]

Within a year, the construction boom intensified with the initiation of another wartime megaproject. To meet the demand for fuel generated by the new Alaska Highway and more particularly by the airports of the Northwest Staging Route, petroleum from the Norman Wells oilfields was to be piped over the Mackenzie Mountains to a refinery in Whitehorse. Work on the Canol Project commenced in 1943. Once again, Whitehorse was a key site in handling equipment and personnel.

Thousands of soldiers and civilian workers flooded into the territory via the White Pass train. To accommodate the many tons of freight and thousands of passengers, the railway schedule was stepped up from one train a week to as many as 25 trains a day. Finally, on October 1st, 1942, the American army leased the railway from White Pass and took charge of its operation until the end of the war. The 770th Railway Battalion joined the existing train crews in keeping the trains running and the line open.

The BYNCo. fleet experienced the same pressure to handle ever greater volumes of freight. Barrels of fuel, vehicles, road-building equipment and lengths of pipeline

*Locomotive #71 derailed in front of the depot, October 22, 1942.*
*" Found with one set of wheels on the roadbed, but not on the rails and the other buried deep in the heart of Texas."—Whitehorse Star*
Yukon Archives / Finnie Collection

were included in the cargo shipped to construction camps at Johnson's Crossing, Teslin, and north to Alaska. Even the T&D boat, *Yukon Rose*, was pressed into military service. The steamers were considered so crucial to the war effort that over the winter of 1942–43, they were hidden away in a slough just south of Lake Laberge. It was feared that if the Japanese bombed Whitehorse, the shipyards would be a prime target.[40]

The American army made its mark on the waterfront. The U.S. Army Corps of Engineers was given "permission to occupy" 150 feet of the riverbank to establish a float plane base down at the present site of Moccasin Flats. Only one of its buildings, now a residence, remains today. Beside it stands a beacon pole that once held a windsock.[41] Other military and civilian float plane bases dotted the length of the riverfront including a dock in front of the steam laundry.

The army established a large camp for the rail crew in the Wye area at the extreme south end of town. When the roundhouse burned down on Christmas Day 1943, the civilian carpenters and soldiers built a new one within a week. The army also put up a new roundhouse (train shed) behind the ways at the shipyard. The old wooden stiff-legged derrick on the dock in front of the depot was replaced by a new steel structure. As well, the army put an addition on the north end of the depot building about 1943. Just north of the station on Front Street, the army built a concrete latrine for the use of GIs. The building still stands and was used by White Pass to house equipment for the telephone and telegraph worker until the late 1970s.[42]

The constant flow of freight on the train soon proved too much for the storage facilities downtown. Babe Richards, an employee of P. Burns & Co., remembers that the construction camps bought such a great volume of meat that she sold it right off the tracks at a point opposite the Regina Hotel.

The railway line was extended. A rail spur was built in late 1942 to the refinery area (now the Marwell Industrial area) and a loop was constructed to the "PE 10" area behind the present Saan Store and RV park.[43] Much of the freight and most of the passengers were offloaded either further down the line north of downtown or else before the train even reached Whitehorse, at the large construction camp at McCrae. The intersection of Main and Front Streets in front of the railway station was still the centre of town, however, and on Sunday afternoons, civilians and soldiers filled the area to hear the military band concerts.

The Whitehorse scene of 1943 made a great impression on visiting journalists. While some were charmed by the false-front buildings and the romantic hulks of the old steamers rotting in the "boneyard" at the shipyards, the predominant sense was of overcrowding and chaos. A small community with a year-round population of about 350 struggled to accommodate some 20,000 new arrivals. Hotel rooms were rented out in shifts, people slept aboard whichever sternwheelers were tied up at the docks, and others bunked down on the station floor. A group of weary Atlinites, en route to Prince Rupert to testify in a murder trial, ended up walking the streets for 48 hours until they could catch their train.

*Civilian workers at Whitehorse depot, ca. 1943.*
Yukon Archives/Preston Collection

It was during this time that existing squatter areas swelled into sizeable communities. When Whiskey Flats filled up, people moved further down the riverbank to the Shipyards, Moccasin Flats and Sleepy Hollow. While these sprawling neighbourhoods had little in the way of services, most of town was in the same situation. Streets were unpaved. A few homes had wells but most people obtained their water from a delivery service. Sewer systems were primitive, for the most part outhouses and septic pits.

As with the rest of the town's residents, the squatters included a variety of types. Of course there were many construction workers. Both First Nations and non-native Yukoners, seeking jobs, moved to town from settlements bypassed by the construction boom. Many of these people found accommodation on the Whitehorse waterfront.

The major construction phase of the Alaska Highway and the Canol Project lasted only a few years but these wartime megaprojects left permanent marks on the Yukon economy, political structure and society. The great influx of outsiders brought several negative repercussions, particularly to First Nations people. Many are still coming to terms with the changes of that era: the introduction of new, often fatal, diseases; problems caused by the ready availability of alcohol; and for many, the end of a traditional lifestyle.

The construction of the highway shifted economic power from Dawson City and Mayo to the southern Yukon. In recognition of this, the political centre shifted as well. The territorial capital was moved from Dawson to Whitehorse in 1953. Whitehorse entered a new era of prosperity based on the highway and the Canadian military personnel who maintained it. The town had grown out of the flat by the river. Within a short time, Whitehorse would turn away from the waterfront as it embraced the changes introduced by the highway.

*U.S. Army military band puts on a Sunday concert for Whitehorse residents, 1942.*
Yukon Archives / Pepper Collection

# THE WATERFRONT
# LEGACY

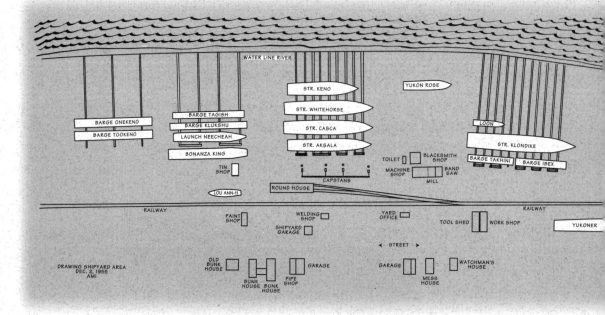

*Adaptation of a drawing showing the shipyards
at the end of the sternwheeler era, December 2, 1955.*
White Pass Transportation Ltd. Corporate Records

## THE END OF AN ERA:
## DEATH OF THE SHIPYARDS

While White Pass executives had initially fought northern lobby efforts for a highway from Alaska to southern Canada and the Lower 48, they quickly adjusted to the possibilities of the highway's presence. By 1946, the BYNCo. had established a bus service and financed a number of highway lodges and gas stations at strategic intervals along the Canadian section of the Alaska Highway. Within a few years, it had also set up a trucking division.

The construction of an all-weather highway to Mayo in 1950 meant the end of the sternwheeler era. For a time, efforts were made to run the *Klondike* on tourist excursions to Lake Laberge but this proved unsuccessful. The BYNCo. shut down its River Division in 1955 after the road was completed to Dawson City.

In the early 1950s, there were 19 assorted buildings and structures associated with the shipyards, excluding the capstans and ways. In December 1955, the shipyard housed seven steamers, four gas boats, and six barges.[44] Within 20 years, all this would be gone. The shipyard buildings were torn down about 1956-57. In the early 1960s, the warehouses and docks by the railway station were also dismantled. There was no further need for transshipment to the riverboats and the old structures could not be adapted to modern freight handling methods such as forklift operations.[45]

The sternwheelers and smaller boats had formed a mobile part of the architectural mosaic of the waterfront for over 50 years. They were as much a part of the structural history of the riverside as the railway station and squatters' shacks. More than that, these vessels were and are part of the identity of the town. The City of Whitehorse uses the image of a sternwheeler in its logo. Along with the docks and warehouses, however, the steamers had become obsolete—anachronisms no longer worth operating.

The boats gradually dispersed. The *Yukon Rose* now sits in a Dawson City backyard. The *Aksala* was moved to the Alaska Highway south of Whitehorse where for many years it marked the entrance to the Paddlewheel Village. Finally the decaying structure was condemned as unsafe and it was dismantled and removed, except for the paddlewheel. Otherwise, all that remains of the vessel is some machinery stored in a government yard. For many years, the *Neecheah* was a restaurant; it now sits in front of the Yukon Transportation Museum. While the *Klondike* is enshrined as a National Historic Site, the hard-working gas boat, the *Loon*, lies mouldering in a Parks Canada warehouse.

By the early 1970s, only two sternwheelers remained on the shipyard ways, the *Whitehorse* and the *Casca*. Despite a chainlink fence and other security measures,

# THE LAST VOYAGE OF THE *S.S. KENO*

The last sternwheeler to travel the Yukon River steamed away from the Whitehorse shipyards on August 25th, 1960. The *Keno* was bound for Dawson City where it would be set up on the riverbank as a Parks Canada historic attraction. The vessel had been refitted for the trip using parts cannibalized from the *Klondike*, the *Casca* and the *Yukon*. Some special arrangements were necessary: the pilot house was removed to the boat deck and the stacks were hinged so the boat could fit under the bridge at Carmacks. As there were no more wood camps, the boat carried its own firewood for fuel. Three crew members were Yukon riverboat veterans: Frank Slim was the pilot, Henry Breaden was the first mate and Len Bath was the fireman. The captain, John Blakely, came from Radium Hot Springs and the remainder of the crew were "greenhorns." The boat ran aground at Slackwater Crossing above Minto; otherwise it was a smooth trip. At the end of the four-day voyage, the *Keno* arrived to a boisterous welcome from the entire population of Dawson, all waiting on the riverbank.

*The S.S. Keno was one of the smaller BYN sternwheelers, built for the shallower waters of the Stewart River. Here the vessel is docked at Stewart Island where ore sacks from Mayo will be transshipped to a larger vessel.*

Yukon Archives / GSC Collection

**The Whitehorse and the Casca in the early 1970s.**
*Yukon Archives / Hadden Collection*

someone managed to get aboard and light a fire. On the 20th of June 1974, the two sternwheelers went up in flames and were totally demolished. Once the wreckage was cleared away, nothing remained of the British Yukon Navigation Company Shipyards.

*The Whitehorse*
*and the Casca*
*go up in flames,*
*June 20, 1974.*

Whitehorse Star photo

# THOSE PESKY SQUATTERS

In 1950, Whitehorse was incorporated as a city and finally able to govern its own affairs. Formerly the city carried out its municipal housekeeping through the Territorial Council. After the Yukon's capital moved from Dawson, Whitehorse became the centre for three levels of government: federal, territorial and municipal. This proved to be a major drawback when it came to dealing with issues such as squatter relocation. The various levels of jurisdiction, not to mention land ownership, often overlapped requiring federal, territorial, and municipal agreement on policies and approaches. Unanimous agreement by all three parties was rare. The cooperation of the town's largest business, White Pass, was also required, as many squatters occupied its property.

*Whiskey Flats in its heyday.*
*Whitehorse Star photo*

A squatter is "one who occupies, or whose goods occupy a building on land to which he, or the owner of the building does not have legal title."[46] Legally, the squatters had no right to the land under their buildings, though they did hold title to any removable property on the land, that is, the buildings.

By the mid 1950s, the city administration and White Pass agreed that the squatters should be removed, particularly from the Whiskey Flats area. With the construction of the Robert Campbell Bridge to the new suburb of Riverdale in 1957, the Flats were no longer on the town's fringes. Riverdale commuters, annoyed by the view from the bridge, lobbied to clean up the squatter community. At the same time, the government of Canada agreed to move a number of the beached sternwheelers to South Whiskey Flats as the nucleus of a park. White Pass donated the land under North Whiskey Flats to the Rotary Club for a city park. All that was needed was to somehow dispose of the squatters. Most Whiskey Flats residents, however, were quite happy where they were and unwilling to move without some form of compensation.

The waterfront squatter communities had acquired a wartime reputation as unsavoury areas, peopled by transients and noted for partying and bootlegging. While there was some truth in this assertion, few realize that in 1956 the squatters comprised a third of the lower townsite population and contributed significantly to the town's economy.

At the outset of the squatter eviction movement, there were 342 people living in Whiskey Flats and 772 in Moccasin Flats.[47] A high proportion of these people were of Aboriginal ancestry. Many well-known Whitehorse and Yukon residents lived in one of these communities at one time. Nearly 70 per cent of the squatters owned their own homes. At the time, Whitehorse was experiencing a housing shortage. Rents were high and much of the available housing was substandard. Squatting was con-

sidered a legitimate option for either getting by on a low income or getting ahead by avoiding high housing costs.

By the time the various government bodies finally took action to remove the squatters, most felt they had acquired certain rights. A number of squatters paid taxes. Many people had applied for leases or title to the property under their structures. These applications were kept on file for a number of years despite a federal policy not to allow development within the 100-foot crown reserve along a waterway. Many squatters filed an application and then proceeded to build with no government objections. This inaction was seen as acceptance, if not approval, of the squatters' presence.

After amending the *Territorial Lands Act* in 1957, the government could legally evict squatters. If a squatter failed to comply with an eviction notice, however, forcible removal could be construed as assault. In one case, an eviction notice served on a squatter resulted in several years' worth of court battles. During that time, the squatter continued to reside in Moccasin Flats.[48]

In the late 1950s and 1960s, the Yukon government employed a variety of tactics in its attempt to clear the squatter areas. While most of these stratagems focused on clearing South Whiskey Flats (now the *S.S. Klondike* National Historic Site) and later North Whiskey Flats (now Rotary Peace Park), they were also applied to many squatters in the Shipyards, Moccasin Flats, and Sleepy Hollow.

As early as 1956, it was recognized that squatter removal would not work unless an alternate relocation site was available. In the early 1960s, a number of undeveloped lots were opened up along the Alaska Highway in the new subdivisions of Porter Creek, Crestview, McCrae, and Canyon Crescent. These locations, far from the city centre, were not a viable alternative for most downtown squatters.

Consequently, the various levels of government and White Pass came to an arrangement whereby, with federal assistance, the municipality would buy from White Pass a large block of downtown property for squatter relocation. Most squatters, White Pass, and the three government bodies approved. Whitehorse voters disagreed, however, based on an assumption that somehow the squatters were getting a good deal at taxpayers' expense. The proposal was defeated in two successive plebiscites in 1961 and 1962. The squatters then attempted to raise the purchase price of Lot 19 but could raise only $12,000 of the required $17,800.

The city established the "Transient Area" in the northern part of town in what is now the Marwell industrial area. Buildings that were considered below the standard acceptable for the new subdivisions were moved here. The Transient Area was established about 1961 but was in use until well into the 1970s.

In 1962, the territorial government offered to move squatter buildings free of charge to any owned or leased lot within a ten mile radius of the city. Simultaneously, it announced that all unoccupied buildings would be removed. In the same year, the federal government set aside funds to finance squatter relocation, a program that continued until 1969. The combined tactics of negotiating removal and relocation terms with individual squatters and summary removal of unused structures

*North end of Shipyards community, 1992.*
*Midnight Arts photo*

continued over the next seven years. The incentive of a new park and historic site prompted community groups to assist in the clean-up.

White Pass dealt directly with the squatters in 1968, when it negotiated relocations from land that became the Second Avenue extension, and again in 1975, when the company attempted to clear the Shipyards area.[49]

By the late 1970s, the territorial government was examining the squatter issue throughout the Yukon. An effective squatter policy required federal cooperation, however, as many squatters were on crown land or land reserved under Aboriginal land claims. Finally, in 1986 the government issued a draft policy for public input. In 1987, the final policy came out and squatters could apply for the land under their structures.

The residents of Sleepy Hollow and the Shipyards elected to make a group presentation to the Squatter Review Panel. Tom Munson, a Shipyards resident, spoke for the group which wanted to be dealt with as part of the Aboriginal land claims process. Supporting statements were read by Ed Schultz of Kwanlin Dun First Nation, Linda Johnson of the Yukon Historical & Museums Association and Margaret Joe, the area Member of the Legislative Assembly.[50] Subsequently, most squatters were offered lifetime leases to their structures. The issue is still unresolved pending Aboriginal land claims in the area.

According to some, squatting was never the real problem. Difficulties arose only when the land occupied by squatters was required for other purposes, or squatter areas were identified as a community blight. Interestingly, the squatter removal program of the late 1950s and 1960s lost much of its impetus once North and South Whiskey Flats were cleared. Squatters continued to occupy the peripheral areas of the Shipyards, Moccasin Flats and Sleepy Hollow.

# WATERFRONT DEVELOPMENT

The first step in the redevelopment of the Whitehorse waterfront for public use was the removal of the squatters from Whiskey Flats in the 1960s. This was done in order to establish an historic park around one of the beached White Pass sternwheelers and create a tourist attraction. The 1963 City of Whitehorse Metropolitan Plan had recommended the relocation, the rationale

*Whitehorse Star photo*

being that…*features such as the Sternwheeler and Museum are sited in unattractive and relatively unaccessible areas.*[51]

At that time the city museum, now the MacBride Museum, was located in one of the town's oldest buildings, the small log telegraph building on the corner of First and Steele. It says much for the re-orientation of the downtown area that a structure one block from the White Pass station should be perceived as "relatively unaccessible."

In 1966, the *Klondike* was transported from the shipyards to a new site in what had been South Whiskey Flats. This proved to be a tremendous exercise in logistics. Using three bulldozers and eight tons of Palmolive Princess soap, a crew of 12 took three weeks to tow the boat through downtown streets to its new location. The boat was gradually restored during the 1970s and on July 1st, 1981, it was declared a National Historic Site.[52] A few years after the *Klondike* had been moved,

*The Klondike makes its last voyage down First Avenue to a new resting place at South Whiskey Flats, 1966.*
Whitehorse Star photo

the Rotary Club spearheaded the campaign to clear the remainder of Whiskey Flats to establish a city park.

About 1970, the Canadian and American parks services began negotiating the establishment of the Klondike Gold Rush International Historic Park. This ambitious concept was proposed to encompass the entire Klondike Gold Rush route from Seattle to Dawson City. Significant sites along the route such as the Chilkoot Pass, Bennett, Whitehorse and Dawson would be commemorated and interpreted. It is likely that the Chilkoot Pass will be commemorated under this program in the near future. Parks officials are unable to say what implications there are, if any, for the Whitehorse waterfront.

Through the 1970s and 1980s, a number of waterfront planning documents were prepared. For a few years, in the mid 1980s, the city even hired its own Waterfront Development Officer.[53] All these plans were hamstrung by the fact that the city owned none of the property along the waterfront. As part of a large block land transfer in 1970, control of the 100-foot reserve along the riverbank passed from the federal to the territorial government.[54] With the exception of a lease under the old 20-20 site, the remainder belonged to White Pass.

Another factor affecting waterfront planning was the persistence of the squatter communities, despite the various efforts to relocate or evict them. One planning document even suggested that the Shipyards squatters be left "relatively intact" and the plan developed around them. City council took exception to this suggestion, fearing that taxpayers might have to bear the burden for renovations to squatter areas.[55]

Over the past decade, there have been a number of events affecting the waterfront. In 1982, the White Pass and Yukon Railway closed its service between Whitehorse and Skagway. For a few years, there were various efforts to buy and reactivate the railway. The company now runs a summer tourist operation between Skagway and the White Pass summit. Extension of the service to Whitehorse has not been economically feasible to date, and appears increasingly unlikely for the future. Without the railway running along the waterfront, one of the few remaining business attractions is gone.

The Yukon government increased its interests in the waterfront by acquiring more land there. In 1987, the territorial government purchased the Southerly Islands from White Pass. Since then, Kishwoot Island, the largest island in this block, has been developed into a recreational area with assistance from the Canadian Army which built the footbridge and the Yukon Outdoors Club, which has maintained the site since 1989 under the Adopt-a-Park program.[56]

In 1991, the Yukon government bought additional White Pass land. This substantial amount of waterfront property extended from the territorial administration building to the south, to a point downriver from Strickland Street to the north. That same year also saw the commencement of the controversial Taga Ku project. This large development, initiated by the Champagne Aishihik First Nation, was to include two office towers and a five-star Holiday Inn. The project was shelved because the succeeding government withdrew its support. The squatters continue to live on the riverbank and there is still no consensus on the future of the waterfront.

*Until the early 1980s, the waterfront came to life every February during the*
*Yukon Sourdough Rendezvous celebration.*
Yukon Archives / Yukon Sourdough Rendezvous Collection

# CONCLUSION

Compared to the bustling river and rail terminus of the first half of the century, the waterfront now seems relatively deserted. Few buildings or features remain to bear witness to its vital past. Still, all the major forms of transportation in the Yukon are depicted in the history of the waterfront. Whitehorse, and the riverbank in particular, was the Yukon's transportation nexus. Whitehorse was established because of a navigation hazard. Its role as the head of navigation on the Yukon River continued to be the town's raison d'être until the construction of the Alaska Highway.

Where river navigation stopped, the rail began. Whitehorse was the end of steel for the railway that served as the main land link to the Outside. This was also the starting point of the Overland Trail to Dawson, and a jumping off point for land routes to Kluane and other spots not serviced by water. The railyards were the distribution point for the workers and equipment that built the Alaska Highway, the Yukon's most prominent land route. The banks of the river even served as a harbour for aircraft when air travel in the territory was in its infancy.

*Steamer Whitehorse being loaded at the dock, 1948.*
*Yukon Archives / Bennett Collection*

The pattern and type of buildings along the waterfront give us insight into the way Whitehorse, and the Yukon's river communities in general, were settled. A wide variety of functional types are still here to be seen: crude shacks, tidy train crew's houses, stark industrial structures, public services and, of course, one of the Yukon's two railway stations, the other being in Carcross. The pattern of settlement is written in the history of these buildings: the White Pass setting the stage with its station and yards, wharfage and warehouses; the dependent and supportive industries that grew up around the transportation locus, including shipyards, stockyards, lumber companies, merchants and laundries; and finally, the riverfront inhabitants, legitimate or not, who both supported and lived from the river and its associated industries.

The politics of settling the waterfront gives us insight into the social, political and economic forces at work in the creation of the town. The railway, local politicians, the Crown, First Nations people, squatters, small business, and big merchants all were ingredients in the simmering, often boiling, stewpot of the waterfront. Nowhere else was there such a dynamic and diverse set of influences at work.

*View of the Shipyards community, 1992.*
Midnight Arts photo

While it is not always a savoury or glamorous story, or the scene of grand events set against stately architecture, the edge of the river was clearly the stage for the forces and resources that formed the heart of the city.

*View of the waterfront looking downriver toward*
*the White Horse Steam Laundry, ca. 1904.*
British Columbia Archives 20074

# THE WATERFRONT TODAY

## WALKING ON THE EDGE:
## AN HISTORICAL WALKING TOUR

The area we have described as "the waterfront" in this book covers a considerable amount of territory. Fortunately, it is best viewed in short segments. All of the sites described here are on flat terrain and easy to walk. You can go for a ten minute hike along First Avenue, or spend half a day and take it all in. We invite you to take along this book and go for a tour along the edge of the river. Use the map at the front of the book as well.

A good place to start is Miles Canyon. Here you can get a feel for the treacherous waters that were the reason Whitehorse was established. Miles Canyon can be

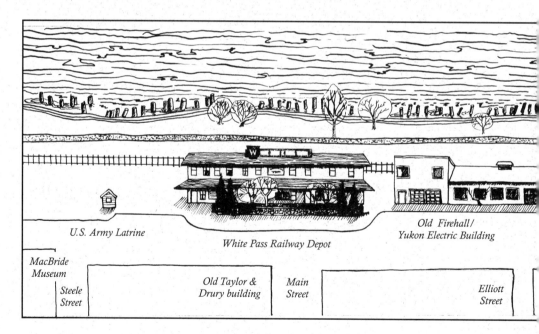

U.S. Army Latrine

White Pass Railway Depot

Old Firehall /
Yukon Electric Building

MacBride
Museum

Steele
Street

Old Taylor &
Drury building

Main
Street

Elliott
Street

reached by car (motor homes not recommended), following the signs from the Alaska Highway or the South Access Road. After crossing the foot bridge to the east side of the Yukon River and a short climb, more adventurous hikers can walk upriver (south) along the tops of the rugged basalt canyon walls about three kilometres to the former site of Canyon City. While it is a moderately easy walk, the trail does follow the edge of the cliffs and should not be attempted by those with vertigo. Alternately, the easier gradient of the old tramway roadbed is further inland and runs through mixed coniferous forest to the site from near the Chadburn Lake Road.

A good, if wiggly, road will take you from the Canyon, along Schwatka Lake to the hydro dam where you join the South Access Road into town. During low water, the remains of the *S.S. Canadian* can be seen as one drives or walks the South Access. There is no room for cars to stop, so extended viewing is not recommended.

Once you have entered town, you can park at the *S.S. Klondike* National Historic Site or further on at Rotary Peace Park across Second Avenue. Well-kept pathways will lead you along the riverbank from either place to the north end of downtown.

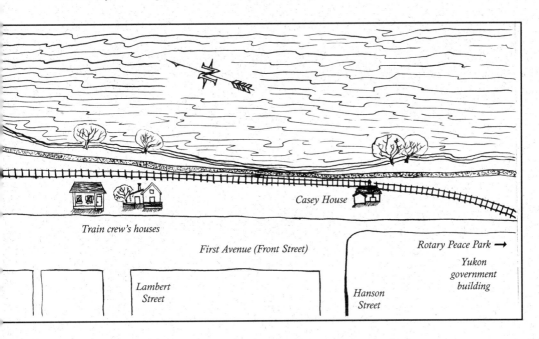

Train crew's houses

Casey House

First Avenue (Front Street)

Rotary Peace Park →

Lambert Street

Hanson Street

Yukon government building

The map on the previous page takes you from the Casey House, near the Yukon government building, to the downstream side of the White Pass Station. Then you will be just across the street from the MacBride Museum which contains excellent photographs and exhibits on early Whitehorse, and rail and river travel. From the museum, make your way back via First and Second Avenue or retrace your steps along the water. Or you may choose to continue walking along the railway north to the old shipyards area and the roundhouse. While there are only a few historic buildings in this stretch, one can still see the wharf pilings and scraps of ship hardware all along the shore.

We have not provided a map of the Shipyards community. The houses in the Shipyards are private homes and we request that readers not intrude on the privacy of the residents. This final segment of the waterfront can be seen from Kishwoot Island, which can be reached via Second Avenue, just where it curves west to join Fourth Avenue. The island itself has well-established trails and makes a pleasant walk through a riverine environment.

*Overhead view of the sunken S.S. Canadian.*
*A. Hedstrom photo*

# S.S. CANADIAN

During low water, one can see a rusted metal hulk sticking out of the Yukon River by the bend upriver of the *S.S. Klondike*. This is an old riverboat boiler, marking the remains of the steamer *Canadian*.

The *S.S. Canadian*, built in Victoria in 1898, travelled north to the Klondike Gold Rush via the Alaskan coast and up the lower Yukon River to Dawson. It was originally operated by the Canadian Development Company, then sold to the British Yukon Navigation Company in 1901.

In 1938, fire damaged the vessel's stern. At the same time, the riverbank south of town was washing away under the railway tracks. The *Canadian* was deliberately sunk here to create a breakwater, allowing a new channel to be dredged out.[57]

# *S.S. KLONDIKE* NATIONAL HISTORIC SITE

In 1929, the British Yukon Navigation Company built the sternwheeler *Klondike* in the Whitehorse shipyards as a cargo vessel. Its unique design provided 50 per

***Stern view of the Klondike II by the shipyards, 1938.***
*Yukon Archives / GSC Collection*

cent greater freight capacity without losing the shallow draft necessary to navigate the bars and shifting channels of the Yukon River. The vessel could handle over 272 tonnes (300 tons) without pushing a barge. For the next six years, the *Klondike* transported passengers and general cargo downstream to Dawson, and silver-lead ore transshipped from Mayo on the upstream trip.

The *Klondike* ran aground in 1936, but the company salvaged its machinery and built an identical boat, the *Klondike II* in 1937. After an all-weather road was built to Mayo in 1950, the sternwheelers were no longer needed to carry cargo. The *Klondike* was refurbished as a cruise ship but this proved uneconomical and the vessel was beached in 1955. The White Pass and Yukon Route donated the *Klondike* to Parks Canada who moved it to this site in 1966 and restored it.[58]

## ROTARY PEACE PARK

The White Pass and Yukon Route donated the land under Whiskey Flats to the Rotary Club of Whitehorse in 1960 on condition that it be used for a park.

By the fall of 1969, North Whiskey Flats had been cleared of its squatter population and the Rotarians began developing the site. Over the next five years, club members arranged for the construction of a playground, a bandstand, washrooms and the landscaping of the site at a cost of approximately $100,000. In 1974, the club presented the completed park to the City of Whitehorse. Rotary Park was renamed Rotary Peace Park in 1993.

*Casey House.*
Midnight Arts photo

## CASEY HOUSE

All along the railway, there were dozens of utility buildings for storing equipment and materials used by section crews in the maintenance and operation of the railway. A casey car was housed here. Casey cars were small, gas-powered rail trucks that transported crews to their work sites.

The vintage of the structure is unknown though its design and shiplap siding would place it before 1950. It was likely that it was moved onto this site and had previously served a different purpose. According to one source, it may have been the residence of the railway section foreman and was moved here from Whiskey Flats. The building features a set of double doors track-side to allow ease of access for the car.

# TRAIN CREW'S HOUSES

Photographs from the mid-1950s show small houses on this site. This type of dwelling was once quite common. They were built by the dock and train workers, often

*One of the train crew's houses.*
*Midnight Arts photo*

illegally, on White Pass property. The upstream building (pictured on the left) is likely the last remaining structure of this type. The downstream building (below) is a more recent import. Its pan abode style of construction makes it likely that it post-dates 1955.

While unremarkable architecturally, functionally these structures represent a notable characteristic of rail and boat workers' housing. They are a minimal sort of habitation, but more substantial than many squatters' residences. These particular buildings were either built by White Pass or constructed with their blessing. At the time of writing, the houses are owned by the Government of the Yukon. They have been boarded up and sit empty pending a decision on a waterfront plan for the City (see also page 25).

*Another of the train crew's houses,*
*likely built after 1955.*
*Midnight Arts photo*

# FIRE HALL

Whitehorse's first fire department, like many of the new town's services, was organized by the Board of Trade with the support of the Territorial Council. The firefighters were all volunteer. By October 1901, the new Fire Hall, a handsome frame building notable for its hose-drying tower, had been completed.[59] The fire hall's central location proved of little use during the great fire of May 1905. The pump and water supply failed and within two hours, fire destroyed much of the downtown core (see page 26).

The town immediately began rebuilding. Within a few days, many businesses had re-opened in tents until more permanent structures could be constructed.[60] Fire protection improved when the Yukon Electrical Company moved next to the fire station.

Thirty years later, another fire almost destroyed the fire station itself. Sparks from the Y.E.C. boiler ignited the fire tower. The firefighters subdued the blaze before it could reach the boiler room but the roof and fire tower were destroyed. By the summer of 1935, the Y.E.C. had ordered a 110-volt diesel electric plant and the Fire Hall was renovated. The hose tower was removed, the roof raised four feet, and the upstairs living quarters enlarged.[61]

In 1949, the fire department moved to a new building on Steele Street.

# YUKON ELECTRICAL CO.

In the summer of 1900, a group of entrepreneurs announced they were planning to obtain a franchise for an electric light plant. By the following year, the Yukon Electrical Company had set up business on the riverfront north of the Whitehorse Steam Laundry. It provided a limited service, supplying power for electric lighting to businesses and residences during certain hours of the day.

*The former firehall/*
*Yukon Electrical Co. building.*
Midnight Arts photo

After the great fire of 1905 destroyed much of the downtown core, the

Yukon Electrical Company relocated to the south side of the Fire Hall, transporting their building on railway flat cars. In addition to their existing electrical service, the company contracted to support Fire Hall operations with a pumping station containing two steam pumps and a boiler.[62]

After the fire station moved to a new site in 1949, this building was largely rebuilt although some elements remain of the original structure. Eventually, the company's offices moved to a larger building across the street.

In the late 1970s, White Pass purchased Yukon Electrical's interest in the waterfront building. After installing gyprock and shelves, they stored office records here until early 1992.[63] The remainder of the building was also used for storage by various community groups. The structure now belongs to the Yukon government.

## RAILWAY DEPOT

The original railway station was a simple but elegant building featuring a bellcast hip roof and dormers. The main floor of the depot housed the customs office and various rail functions. The ticket agent and his family lived upstairs.

Although it was one of the first buildings to give the town an aura of permanence, its own lifespan was short. During the fire of May 23rd, 1905, the railway station was one of many downtown buildings destroyed. Employees managed to save most of the station books, records, express and bonded goods, but Agent Mellot and his family lost all their personal possessions (see page 26).

*WP&YR station.*
*Midnight Arts photo*

Within a few days, however, White Pass started to construct a new depot building. By late July, they had moved in. Company management took the opportunity to plan a number of building improvements. The new station had a cellar housing a well and furnace, the main floor area was rearranged to allow for larger offices and a reduced waiting area, and the living quarters were re-established upstairs. The whole building was pronounced "better arranged and more comfortable."[64]

The station stood in this form until 1943 when it was expanded due to the huge increase in railway use. There was little attempt made to preserve the lines or appearance of the original station. The sweeping roof lines were replaced with a medium gable roof covering an enlarged second storey. Split log or "Mohawk" siding was added to the station in the 1950s. The depot has gradually seen a shift in function from station to office building as the fortunes and functions of the railway company changed. Little is discernible of the original floor layout; the interior is now almost entirely offices.

*Seeing off a sternwheeler, 1938. Note the wharf pilings, many of which are still there today.*
*Yukon Archives/GSC Collection*

Despite the alterations, this structure is the end of steel and one of only two railway stations in the Yukon. The site has served as an anchor to Main Street and the town since the first station was constructed in 1900. It is not only an integral part of the waterfront, it is the crucial intersection of two landscapes—the city and the river's edge.

# U.S. ARMY LATRINE

This little concrete structure sits just north of the station. It was constructed as a public toilet for the use of the American troops building the Alaska Highway and may be unique in the Yukon both functionally and architecturally.

Permafrost makes the use of poured concrete a risky business in the north, as the high density of the material tends to make it sink and crack when the frozen ground shifts and heaves. As a result, few buildings in the Yukon

*A relic of the American army,*
*the concrete latrine.*
Midnight Arts photo

were built with concrete foundations, let alone concrete walls. Concrete was a fairly safe material for this facility because it is too small to have much weight and it sits on a stable piece of ground.

Other than the wooden structures built in construction camps, we know of no other washroom facility built expressly for army use. This enduring structure of dubious distinction was later used by White Pass for storage.

# ROUNDHOUSE

This is the only remaining WP&YR roundhouse in Canada. It was built in 1943, after the original, located in the Wye area, burned down. Although it is more properly a train shed, since trains backed out rather than being turned around, it nonetheless served the same function and was known locally as the roundhouse. The main yards and repair facilities for WP&YR were in Skagway, Alaska but, as

*The roundhouse or train shed. The east wall was blackened by flames from the burning of the Whitehorse and the Casca in 1974.*
Midnight Arts photo

the end of steel, Whitehorse also required a repair and maintenance facility. The roundhouse was associated with the shipyards and the maintenance and operations end of the railway business. Industrial sites such as this are uncommon in the Yukon. Over the years, the few breweries, mills, and fabrication shops that were built have almost entirely disappeared.

# MYSTERIES IN THE SHIPYARDS

All along the waterfront, building construction dates and even places of origin are something of a mystery. Some attempts were made to map the squatter areas and keep records for tax assessments. These maps are of little help, however, since the buildings were periodically cleared away and just as rapidly new ones were constructed. Buildings, such as the Sewell Cabin and the Pioneer Hotel, are distinctive enough that they are fairly easy to identify by rough measurement, location and written description. This is not the case with the majority of squatter structures. Most have been moved, torn down and replaced, modified or brought in from other locations.

The landscape kept changing and does to this day. While this means that there is little left that is old or original to the site, we have to consider this dynamic aspect of the waterfront as part of its historic character. Buildings which were built after 1955 were not described nor were those structures which were determined to remain anonymous and refused to give up any history.

# SEWELL CABIN

When Whitehorse was first established, it was a tent town. These inexpensive structures could be erected quickly for temporary dwellings and places of business.

Sometimes the transition between tent and permanent structure was not sharply defined. In a process akin to a snail building up its shell from the inside, many tents were transformed into frame or log structures, without ever taking the tent down. These buildings usually have a characteristic appearance of a wooden walltent. The Sewell Cabin is one such building. Following a fire in the cabin some years ago, canvas was found between the inner and outer walls (see also page 30).[65]

*The Sewell Cabin.*
Midnight Arts photo

While this was once a common type of structure in Whitehorse, most of these metamorphosed tent buildings are now gone. The Sewell Cabin is all the more interesting in that it can be dated to early in the century.

The building is important due to its age, its vernacular architecture—a remnant from an earlier Whitehorse—and its association with a number of notable Yukoners. Past residents of this building include Frank Slim, well-known riverboat pilot, and Louis Irvine, a cat train operator and one of the first drivers to bring a bus over the Alaska Highway.[66]

# MILLER HOUSE

The American Army probably built a number of structures along the waterfront during the construction of the Alaska Highway. This building was apparently an office associated with their float plane dock.

There is little to identify its use from either exterior or interior appearance. The bellcast hipped roof is not typically military. According to Don Miller, the present owner, this building and the Sewell House were the only ones standing on that part of Moccasin Flats when he moved there in the early 1950s.[67]

# RED PIERCY CABIN

Little is known about this single storey, log cabin other than the fact it was occupied by Red Piercy for a number of years. Mr. Piercy was one of only six Canadian pilots during World War II to be decorated for flying "The Hump," the supply route between India and Burma. Don Miller thinks the cabin was built by a sternwheeler crew member. Another local resident, John Hatch, says it was built between 1902 and 1908 by a shipwright working in the shipyards.

# THE PIONEER HOTEL

Sections of this structure, now in the Shipyards area, constitute the remains of what is probably the oldest extant building in Whitehorse.

Ed Dixon, a former NWMP corporal and river pilot, established a number of businesses in the new town of Whitehorse. During the height of the Klondike Gold Rush, Dixon was responsible for safely steering hundreds of boats through the churning waters of Miles Canyon and White Horse Rapids.

Dixon's first enterprise was the erection of the Closeleigh Hotel and Saloon (later renamed the Pioneer Hotel) on Front Street early in 1900. The hotel was situated on the site of the present Closeleigh Manor. Some people say this building was once the Savoy Hotel and had been moved from the original settlement on the east bank of the river.[68] Like many early Whitehorse commercial structures, the hotel was constructed of logs with a framed false front or boom town facade. Later that year, Dixon sold out his interest in this building to his partner John Smart.

***Part of the former Pioneer Hotel.***
*Midnight Arts photo*

Ed Dixon remained involved in Whitehorse affairs. His enterprises included management of the Regina Hotel and the construction of the Whitehorse Steam Laundry. His various civic activities culminated in his election to the Territorial Council in 1915, as the member for Whitehorse. A year later, Dixon enlisted to fight in Europe as a member of George Black's 104th Regiment. After the war, he lived in British Columbia until his death in 1955. His ashes were scattered over Miles Canyon, a ceremony attended by an RCMP honour guard.

Over the years, the building went through a number of owners and a number of additions and alterations. Anna B. Puckett took over the hotel for a few years about 1930. She renovated the run-down Pioneer Rooms.[69] Many White Pass longshore and shipyard workers stayed in this building after it was converted to a rooming house.

In the early 1950s, Taylor Chevrolet bought the hotel property and sold the building to Max Kushner. Mr. Kushner dismantled the structure and moved it to Moccasin Flats. Portions of the building were used to erect three cabins. Mr. Kushner lived

*The Pioneer Hotel on Front Street, May 21, 1903.*
*Yukon Archives 4636/Atlin Historical Society Collection*

in one and rented out the other two. The remainder of the building was used for firewood and salvage. One cabin burned down but two are still in use.[70]

Most of the heritage value of this building was lost when it was removed, in sections, from its original site. These pieces may be, however, the sole remnants of the original town of Whitehorse. It is quite amazing that any of the hotel survived the numerous fires that plagued the downtown core. The structures are prime examples of recycled housing and survivors from Whitehorse's earliest history.

## THE REST

While several squatter residences remain on the waterfront, their history and provenance are blurry. The Sewell Cabin and the Miller House were constructed on site. Others, such as the two cabins incorporating the remains of the Pioneer Hotel, were definitely relocated to this area. Some buildings may have been brought here intact, while others were constructed from salvaged materials.

The primary source of information on these structures is oral history. Even long-time residents of the area could not say with any assurance just when most of the buildings were erected or brought in. In time, the stories of these buildings may be known. Just as likely, though, they will never be. Some of the structures may be just what they seem, cobbled together bits of flotsam on the banks of the Yukon River. On the other hand, this is the oldest residential/industrial area of the city and contains the last vestiges of the settlement's origins. So whether you think the edge of the river is run down and drab, or whether you think it is romantic and evocative, it surely was—and maybe still is—the heart of the city.

*Rendezvous participants on the Yukon River ice, no date.*
*Yukon Archives / Yukon Sourdough Rendezvous Collection*

# END NOTATIONS

[1] Griffith Taylor, "A Yukon Domesday: 1944" in C.A. Dawson, ed., *The New Northwest* (Toronto: University of Toronto Press, 1947), p. 91.

[2] Bison bones found at the mouth of McIntyre Creek have been dated at approximately 6000 years old. Jeff Hunston, Director of Heritage Branch, Government of the Yukon, personal communications, 27 October 1992 and 18 April 1994.

[3] Catharine McClellan, *My Old People Say* (Ottawa: National Museum of Canada, 1975), pp. 31, 189.

[4] Frederick Schwatka, *A Summer in Alaska* (St. Louis, Mo.: J.W. Henry, 1894), pp. 162-170.

[5] Julie Cruikshank, *Dän Dhá Ts'edenintth'é* (Vancouver: Douglas & McIntyre, 1991), pp. 109-110.

[6] Schwatka, *A Summer in Alaska*, p. 165.

[7] In 1984, the First Nation that had been known as the Whitehorse Band altered its name to Kwänlin Dun, Southern Tutchone for "People of the Rapids." C. McClellan, *Part of the Land, Part of the Water* (Vancouver: Douglas & McIntyre, 1987), p. 42.

[8] R. Coutts, *Yukon Places & Names* (Sidney, B.C.: Gray's Publishing Ltd., 1980), pp.183-84, 284-85.

[9] Helene Dobrowolsky, "Miles Canyon/ Macaulay and Hepburn Tramways," in *Study Tour of the Yukon and Alaska* (Ottawa, Society for Industrial Archeology, 1990).

[10] Yukon Archives, YRG I, Series 1, vol. 13, f. 2788: Whitehorse townsite, 1899-1901.

[11] Information for this section was taken from the following sources: Peter Clibbon, *The Evolution and Present Land Use Patterns of Whitehorse, Yukon Territory* (Sainte-Foy, Québec: Université Laval, Centre de recherche en aménagement et en développemente, ca. 1990), p. 5; Paul M. Koroscil, "The Historical Development of Whitehorse: 1898-1945" (*The American Review of Canadian Studies*, Autumn 1988, Vol. XVIII, No. 3) pp. 276-277; White Pass & Yukon Route, Corporate Record Group 1, finding aid, pp. 64-70; and YRG I, Series 1, vol. 12, f. 2647, part A - Whitehorse waterfront, 1902-03; and Series 1, vol. 26, f. 8729 - British Yukon Railway Co., lease 1500 feet, dockage at Whitehorse, 1900–20.

[12] *Dawson Daily News*, 3 April 1900.

[13] *The Yukon Sun*, 22 May 1900.

[14] Sources for this section include: the *Dawson Daily News*, 3 April 1900; *Daily Alaskan*, 22 May, 22 June, 21 August & 14 November, 1900; and Harry Graham, *Across Canada to the Klondyke* (Toronto: Methuen Publications, 1984), p. 66.

[15] The *Daily Klondike News*, 6 August 1900.

[16] Gordon Bennett, *Yukon Transportation: A History* (Ottawa: National Historic Parks, 1978), pp. 64-69; Ken Coates, *Land of the Midnight Sun* (Edmonton: Hurtig Publishers, 1988), p. 199; *Whitehorse Star*, 30 May 1913; and John Scott interview, 17 September 1992.

[17] YRG I, Series 1, vol. 73, f. 42. Whitehorse, waterfront lease by BYNCo., 1901-30.

[18] WP&YR Corporate Records, Yukon Archives. VI–2–D, folder 9, COR 816. Squatters leases, 1908–09.

[19] Mr. John Scott of Whitehorse provided most of the information for this section during a recorded interview on 17 Sept. 1992 as well as several subsequent conversations.

[20] White Pass Transportation Ltd, Corporate Records, Skagway. Information in this section is based on plan nos. L2b, L20r, and a plan from Valuable Document file #70.

[21] Marvin Taylor, president and chief operating officer, White Pass Transportation Ltd., personal communication, 5 October 1992.

[22] John Scott, September 1992.

[23] Julie Cruikshank, *Life Lived Like a Story* (Vancouver: University of British Columbia Press, 1990), pp. 81-84.

[24] Personal communication from the last tenant, Wayne Alleman, November 1992.

[25] *Daily Alaskan*, 23 May 1905; *Atlin Claim*, 27 May 1905.

[26] *Daily Alaskan*, 13 September 1900.

[27] John Scott, 17 September 1992.

[28] C.D. Taylor interview, 13 Sept. 1978, Yukon River Aural History Project.

[29] *Whitehorse Star*, First Annual Edition, 1 May 1901.

[30] *Yukon News*, 18 Nov. 1985.

[31] YRG I, Series 5, Vol 15, f. 861; Babe Richards, personal communication 28 Oct. 1992; Jim Robb, *The Colourful Five Per Cent*, Vol. 1 (Whitehorse: The Colourful Five Per Cent Co. Ltd., 1984), p. 13.

[32] White Pass Corporate Records, V.D. No. 70; Babe Richards: taped interview, 7 Jan. 1991; personal communication 15 Oct. 1992; Marvin Taylor, 5 Oct. 1992.

[33] Don Miller, personal communication, 6 October 1992; Ella LeGresley, personal communication 16 November 1992.

[34] *Whitehorse Star*, 5 Dec. 1973, 13 May 1971; Yukon River Aural History Project: notes from Henry Breaden, George Dawson, and Louis Irvine interviews.

[35] Bennett, *Yukon Transportation: A History*, pp. 1908-09.

[36] Canada, Energy Mines and Resources, Whitehorse; CLSR Plan No. 50043.

[37] Ronald A. Keith, *Bush Pilot with a Briefcase* (Toronto: Doubleday, 1972), p. 169.

[38] Bennett, p. 122 and D.M. Bain, *Canadian Pacific Airlines: Its History and Aircraft* (Calgary: Kishorn Publications, 1987), p. 17.

[39] Unless otherwise indicated, the information in this section is taken from: Helene Dobrowolsky, "The Impact of Alaska Highway Construction on Whitehorse," a research paper prepared for the Whitehorse 50th Anniversary Society, Feb. 1991.

[40] Marvin Taylor, 6 October 1992.

[41] YRG I, Series 1, vol. 62, f. 35415; Miller, op. cit.

[42] Taylor, op. cit.

[43] Ibid.

[44] White Pass Transportation Ltd. Corporate Records, Plan Nos. R-1103 and V.D. 292.

[45] Marvin Taylor, op. cit.

[46] Tim and Glenda Wilhelm, "Squatter Relocation: Whitehorse, Yukon Territory," in *The People Outside: Studies of squatters, shacktown and shanty residents and other dwellers on the fringe in Canada* (Ottawa: St. Paul University, 1971), p. 131. Most of the information in this section comes from this article.

[47] J.R. Lotz, "The Squatters of Whitehorse: A Study of the Problems of New Northern Settlements" in *The People Outside: Studies of squatters, shacktown and shanty residents and other dwellers on the fringe in Canada* (Ottawa: Canadian Research Centre for Anthropology, St. Paul University, 1971), pp. 116-117.

[48] Ibid., p. 134 and *Whitehorse Star*, 9 March 1961.

[49] Wilhelm, p. 149.

[50] *Whitehorse Star*, 17 May 1988; Tom Munson, "Five Years in the Shipyards," in *Another Lost Whole Moose Catalogue* (Whitehorse: Lost Moose Publishing, 1991), pp. 3-5.

[51] Quoted in Yukon Archives, MRG I, vol. 986, f. 9: letter from R.B. Hougen to the Mayor and Council, 25 July 1964.

[52] Y.H.M.A., *Whitehorse Heritage Buildings* (Whitehorse, 1983), p. 24.

[53] For a full listing of the various waterfront plans, see the Bibliography prepared by Midnight Arts as a companion document to this study.

[54] Block Land Transfer #1447, Mabel Macyshen, Federal Lands, personal communication, October 1992.

[55] *Whitehorse Star*, 25 September 1985.

[56] Ione Christensen, personal communication, 23 November 1992.

[57] N.A. Easton, *Yukon Underwater Diving Association—Heritage Resources Inventory*, prepared for Government of the Yukon, Heritage Branch, 1986; John M. Mills, *Canadian Coastal and Inland Steam Vessels, 1809-1930* (Providence, Rhode Is., 1979); *Yukon River Aural History Project, 1978*—Laurent Cyr interview.

[58] *S.S. Klondike National Historic Site*, pamphlet issued by Environment Canada, Parks Service.

[59] YRG I, Series 4, vol. 8, f. 235A.

[60] *Daily Alaskan*, 23 May 1905; *Atlin Claim*, 27 May 1905.

[61] *Whitehorse Star*, 1 March, 14 June, 19 July 1935; MacBride Museum: Len Tarka Research File, "Buildings of Whitehorse - Fire Department and Yukon Electrical Co."

[62] *Daily Alaskan*, 8 July 1905; *Whitehorse Star*, 15 & 26 August, 8 September 1905.

[63] Ken Steele, property manager, White Pass Transportation Ltd., personal communication, 5 November 1992.

[64] *Daily Alaskan*, 23 May 1905; *Atlin Claim*, 27 May 1905.

[65] Ella LeGresley, personal communication, November 1992.

[66] Louis Irvine, recorded interview, 7 December 1990; Doris Simpson, recorded interview, 25 September, 1991.

[67] Don Miller, personal communication, October 1992.

[68] George Kellett, "The Houses of Whitehorse," *North, 1968; Yukon News*, 13 May 1981.

[69] Helen Horback, "City's History Lives on in Local Landmarks," *Yukon News*, 13 May 1981.

[70] Most of this information came from MacBride Museum research files, Len Tarka Collection—Pioneer Hotel, folders 1 to 9.